PENGUIN BOOKS

MADNESS

sam sax is a queer jewish writer and educator. He has received fellowships from the National Endowment for the Arts, Lambda Literary, the MacDowell Colony, the Blue Mountain Center, and the James A. Michener Center for Writers. sax was the winner of the 2016 Iowa Review Award, and his poems have appeared in *The American Poetry Review*, *Gulf Coast*, *Ploughshares*, *Poetry*, and other journals. His second collection of poems, *Bury It*, will be published by Wesleyan University Press in 2018.

The National Poetry Series was established in 1978 to ensure the publication of five collections of poetry annually through five participating publishers. The Series is funded annually by Amazon Literary Partnership, Barnes and Noble, Betsy Community Fund, the Gettinger Family Foundation, Bruce Gibney, HarperCollins Publishers, Stephen King, Lannan Foundation, Newman's Own Foundation, News Corp, Anna and Olafur Olafsson, the O. R. Foundation, the PG Family Foundation, the Poetry Foundation, Laura and Robert Sillerman, Amy R. Tan and Louis De Mattei, Elise and Steven Trulaske, and the National Poetry Series Board of Directors.

2016 COMPETITION WINNERS

I Know Your Kind
by William Brewer of Brooklyn, NY
Chosen by Ada Limón for Milkweed Editions

For Want of Water
by Sasha Pimentel of El Paso, TX
Chosen by Gregory Pardlo for Beacon Press

Civil Twilight
by Jeffrey Schultz of Los Angeles, CA
Chosen by David St. John for Ecco

MADNESS
by Sam Sax of Austin, TX
Chosen by Terrance Hayes for Penguin Books

Thaw
by Chelsea Dingman of Tampa, FL
Chosen by Allison Joseph for University of Georgia Press

MADNESS

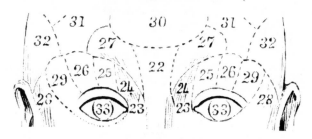

sam sax

PENGUIN BOOKS

PENGUIN BOOKS

An imprint of Penguin Random House LLC
375 Hudson Street
New York, New York 10014
penguin.com

LIBRARY OF CONGRESS CATALOGING-IN-PUBLICATION DATA
Names: Sax, Sam, 1942– author.
Title: Madness / Sam Sax.
Description: New York, New York : Penguin Books, 2017. | Series:
National poetry series
Identifiers: LCCN 2017016060 (print) | LCCN 2017021322 (ebook) |
ISBN 9781524705572 (ebook) | ISBN 9780143131700 (softcover)
Subjects: | BISAC: POETRY / American / General.
Classification: LCC PS3569.A896 (ebook) | LCC PS3569.A896 A6 2017 (print) |
DDC 811/.54—dc23
LC record available at https://lccn.loc.gov/2017016060

Printed in the United States of America
1 3 5 7 9 10 8 6 4 2

Set in Adobe Caslon Pro
Designed by Elyse J. Strongin, Neuwirth & Associates

For my family

Blood & otherwise

פֿאַר ווײַבער און פֿאַר מאַנסבילן וואָס זײַנען אַזוי ווי ווײַבער, דאָס הייסט זיי קענען ניט לערנען

I'm no prophet. My job is making windows where
there were once walls.

—Michel Foucault

When you go crazy, you don't have the slightest
inclination to read anything Foucault ever wrote
about culture and madness.

—Mary Ruefle

CONTENTS

| MADNESS |

NOMENCLATURE

APPENDIX C OF THE *DSM-I* (1952)

SUPPLEMENTARY TERMS OF THE BODY AS A WHOLE (INCLUDING
SUPPLEMENTARY TERMS OF THE PSYCHE AND OF THE BODY
GENERALLY) AND THOSE NOT AFFECTING A PARTICULAR SYSTEM
EXCLUSIVELY

order / disorder

Acarophobia – Acrophobia – Agoraphobia – Antisocialism – Anxiety
– Asthenia – Breath holding – Bruxism – Cachexia – Cancerophobia
– Causalgia – Claustrophobia – Cheiromegaly (enlargement of hands
and fingers) – Chills – Chilly sensations – Collapse – Counting (steps,
etc.) – Cruelty – Deficiency, moral – Dehydration – Delire de toucher
– Depersonalization – Depression – Destructiveness – Diabetes insipidus
– Dipsomania – Disobedience – Edema, hysterical – Edema, other
types – Emotional instability – Enuresis – Erotomania – Facetiousness
– Fatigue, abnormal – Fears, mixed – Feeding problem in children –
Folie du doute – Forgery – Fugue – Gain in weight – Homosexuality –
Hypothermia – Kleptomania – Loss in weight – Mania – Masturbation
– Mendacity pathologic: untruthfulness – Misanthropy – Misogyny –
Moria (Witzelsucht) – Mysophobia – Nail biting – Negativism –
Nymphomania – Obesity – Overactivity – Pain, general – Panic – Panic,
acute homosexual – Paranoid trends – Paroxysmal automatism –
Paroxysmal clouded states – Paroxysmal furor – Paroxysmal psychic
equivalents – Personality, dual – Personality, dissociated – Personality,
paranoid – Personality, schizoid – Personality, syntonic –
Phthisiophobia – Pyrexia; hyperthermia – Pyromania; setting fires –
Quarrelsomeness – Sexual immaturity – Sex offenses – Sexual perversion
– Shock – Simulation, malingering – Somnambulism – Somniloquism
– Stealing – Syncope – Syphilophobia – Tantrums – Tetany – Tetany
due to hyperventilation – Thumb sucking – Tongue swallowing –
Trance – Trichokryptomania – Trichotillomania – Truancy – Urge to
say words – Use of alcohol – Use of drugs – Vagabondage – Vagrancy

SEASONAL AFFECTIVE DISORDER

let's begin with the fields
that line the road
my people fled down
trailed by soldiers
bullets at their heels

o if those fields could speak
surely they'd stay silent

the human coffle
of the barefooted in winter
feet torn to rags
by the graveled ice

i'd like to believe
that spring grew nothing
along the highway

that the flowers weren't
devastating in their beauty

but don't blame biology
for following its own logic

the professor's hand on my neck
that caused me to harden
in my leather

the angel lust of hanged men
erections toward heaven

in america, you can't trust
the flowers

they bloom despite themselves
they blood open
then fall

PSYCHOTHERAPY

after Adélia Prado

i invent three nightmares for my therapist to decipher.

the first i'm eating a plate of boiled peanuts—inside

each a boy, winged + writhing + red, he writhes red

+ winged between my teeth. in the second my father

digs a hole in our backyard, i lie facedown in the rain,

for a moment i'm mud covered, then an island, then a city

swallowed by flood. in the last + this is the most transparent,

i'm a pane of glass all the boys in my class press their lips

against before heading to war. i want my therapist to know,

i'm the war + the glass + the hole + the boiled.

i want him to stab at what's bleeding just below the surface.

to reach down my throat + release me from inside

the locked safe. i want to look at myself in the mirror

without swallowing all my father's heart medicine.

PREDIAGNOSIS

when i was born i felt nothing
but life ripping open before me,
the doctor's white face & coat,
everyone seemed happy i was alive.

but life ripping open before me
led to me ripped open before life.
everyone seemed happy. i was alive
but only for a short time.

me ripped open. before life
i was dependent on milk & men
but only for a short time.
anything can be a drug if you love it.

dependent on milk & men
my overdose a slow child inside me
anyone can be a drug if you love him
all i needed was time.

my overdose a slow-growing child
my man a cancer of light
he said all i needed was time
he left me & i tried to leave life.

my man. my cancer light.
my doctor's white face & coat.
he left me, my life
when i was born i felt everything.

SANCTUARY

my man was committed
to an asylum as a child
          wild thing   fungal
phylum   virus

thought they could fix him
that he could be fixed

his sickness   too much
too much his diagnoses

drugs & boys & language
& boys & drugs

he was given a pill & made old
he was made cold in his skin

i try to place myself
inside the conversion clinic
when i touch his back
as he sleeps

baby queer with bangs
hanged like dead men before his face
arms a collision of scissor wars

& o the shower steam that rose behind him
as his man who was also a child
& also committed
entered him for the first time

between the shifts
of the nurses

took him raw in the open stall
with only the salve of soap
between them blood

i enter him like this
brushing the bodies
from his face
tasting the plastic
restraints

#HYPOCHONDRIA

who were we before germ theory?
back in the liquid days of humors

when tumors grew from an imbalance
in black bile. who were we back

in the miasma days when a bouquet
of dead yellow flowers

below the nose could prevent bacteria
from growing in your spine? thank you

science for teaching me what to fear most.
if i lived two hundred years ago

i'd have been bled nightly, i'd have
slept at the foot of a holy man's bed

i'd have lapped up his snake waters.
on the subway i breathe into my white

t-shirt. i avoid drinking water
when news of brain-eating parasites

surfaces three states away. i recoil
inside my hands when i use them.

i'm trying to be better about being
in the world. what happened?

when i was young i'd make love
to anything with a pulse,

i'd spelunk through sewer veins to find
the easiest way across town. i'd huff paint

& rage until blacking out on a friend's
disgruntled carpet. of course i know

i'm going to die. until then i'm attempting
only to stave off the flies. i'm trading

what's left of my youth for a glass tube
to cast a quiet spell inside.

TRANSORBITAL LOBOTOMY

in through the eye

device adapted from an ice pick

the space between the cornea & tear duct tears

little incisions along the frontal lobe

you open the grapefruit

you open the grape

you open

in the fifties there were tens of thousands performed in the states

sour mess. sour mash. mash-up. macerate.

cut a rug. jitterbug. wonder drug. gutter. tug. suture. lacerate.

erasure. erase. raced. deadened. dead end.

end. replace.

once a doctor removed the frontal lobe of an aggressive ape

what followed was a column of ants

your relative made new & easy to manage

a miracle cure

FEVER THERAPY

give me a chance to create fever and i will cure any disease
—Parmenides

i never knew fevers
            were symptomatic of deeper problems
      they're not what you treat

the body heats the copper pot of your immune system
                        into killing everything not you in you

in those few degrees
            everything

      bacteria & viruses snap into flame as you sweat
      as you in bed a burning planet turning around its burning star

i watch a video of bees swarming an invading hornet, cooking it alive
      inside its yellow & black exoskeleton
                        that's the basic idea

i pull the cursor back to watch the hornet come alive again
      to be covered in insects
                        & again

& further back
they used fevers to treat psychosis

on my desktop, a yellowed photograph of hospital beds
            lined with faces wrapped in dark wet blankets

all our white blood
            cells an oven
                        a coven of bees blushing
a mob hurling
            the winged torch of their young

before knowing he wanted nothing
to do with the insane   my father worked
summers at an asylum in maine

his job was to clean detritus off men
the doctors hardly considered
men

something funny happens
when a person becomes a patient
the name changes & everything
that follows is bandages

ward for the criminally insane
ward of the state   warden
wards off   the wars in your head

there was one man in the corner
who pulled at his nose until his face elongated
into a plague doctor's bird mask

that summer something funny
exposé on the staten island asylum
aired on pbs

patients made human again inside
the camera lens : humans crowded foodless
into dark rooms   humans contorted
into older organisms

dad left his hands behind to study
the history of money

& even robert kennedy called
the place a pit of snakes before
someone shot him in the head.

ON PREP OR ON PRAYER

spare us your burial rites

spare us the first rib
the flood, the resurrection

spare us your dairy & meats
your belief in a life after this one

heaven's a city
we've been priced out of

our mothers fled
for more affordable children
for the price of liver

heaven wants nothing
to do with pleasure
on earth

on this
the occasion of my brother's wedding
i need something awful
done to my body

heaven's a boy
who wants me to crawl
through his mother's midnight-window

heaven's the condom splitting into light

heaven's not a place
more a wound i make & pass through

when we're done
he asks how many men
i've fucked this month
& not loved

spare me the quilt & blanket

spare me the look
in his eyes when he takes me
careful as a poison inside him

spare me the lecture
on the survival
of my body
& i will spare you my body

MEN

APPENDIX C OF THE *DSM-I* (1952)

SUPPLEMENTARY TERMS OF THE BODY AS A WHOLE (INCLUDING
SUPPLEMENTARY TERMS OF THE PSYCHE AND OF THE BODY
GENERALLY) AND THOSE NOT AFFECTING A PARTICULAR SYSTEM
EXCLUSIVELY

order / disorder

Acarophobia – Acrophobia – Agoraphobia – Antisocialism – Anxiety
– Asthenia – Breath holding – Bruxism – Cachexia – Cancerophobia
– Causalgia – Claustrophobia – Cheiromegaly (enlargement of hands
and fingers) – Chills – Chilly sensations – Collapse – Counting (steps,
etc.) – Cruelty – Deficiency, moral – Dehydration – Delire de toucher
– Depersonalization – Depression – Destructiveness – Diabetes insipidus
– Dipsomania – Disobedience – Edema, hysterical – Edema, other
types – Emotional instability – Enuresis – Erotomania – Facetiousness
– Fatigue, abnormal – Fears, mixed – Feeding problem in children –
Folie du doute – Forgery – Fugue – Gain in weight – Homosexuality –
Hypothermia – Kleptomania – Loss in weight – Mania – Masturbation
– Mendacity pathologic: untruthfulness – Misanthropy – Misogyny –
Moria (Witzelsucht) – Mysophobia – Nail biting – Negativism –
Nymphomania – Obesity – Overactivity – Pain, general – Panic – Panic,
acute homosexual – Paranoid trends – Paroxysmal automatism –
Paroxysmal clouded states – Paroxysmal furor – Paroxysmal psychic
equivalents – Personality, dual – Personality, dissociated – Personality,
paranoid – Personality, schizoid – Personality, syntonic –
Phthisiophobia – Pyrexia; hyperthermia – Pyromania; setting fires –
Quarrelsomeness – Sexual immaturity – Sex offenses – Sexual perversion
– Shock – Simulation, malingering – Somnambulism – Somniloquism
– Stealing – Syncope – Syphilophobia – Tantrums – Tetany – Tetany
due to hyperventilation – Thumb sucking – Tongue swallowing –
Trance – Trichokryptomania – Trichotillomania – Truancy – Urge to
say words – Use of alcohol – Use of drugs – Vagabondage – Vagrancy

PSYCHOTHERAPY

the therapist asks the boy to show him on the doll where the man
touched his body. the doll's a smaller boy, dressed in red shorts,
a red mouth & legs. the real boy doesn't want to touch this early
draft, to lead it where he is now, a tan couch in a stale room
in a strip mall off the highway. he points instead to his own body,
huge by comparison, then the wood desk, then up at the water-
stained heaven. this must be the way of things—all signs pointing
toward unknowable destinations. how it was only after,
in the mirror, he saw the drool he'd tongued out of his mouth guard
didn't make him look tough at all, only thirsty & this is why the man
held him down on the mat of the dojang & why his hands spilled &
oiled his small body. the fissure between a sign & its referent
is a faucet opening & closing at once : all the town's road signs worn
illegible after the floods. this is how the boy both welcomed
& unwelcomed the man. how boys become men who make dolls
with their hands. in the locker room after, i stepped out of my white
uniform & was still a child & unquenchable & wanted the man
to follow me in, move my limbs around, fill me with cotton. & when
he didn't, i dressed. this is the memory that flashes on & off in
my head when i think of desire's rotted blood root : like a neighbor's
window you stare at praying to finally see the old woman undressing
then she enters & puts a gun in her mouth.

DIAGNOSIS

we should have you
committed

                   we should have asked
                   what's wrong

no commandment
handed down

                   makes sense
                   from the chaos

i mistake the satellites
for comets   pause

                   a comma hurtling
                   through the black

my mind a little metal
satellite hoarding

                   boring data, always
                   in orbit around

the flies   pause
we should have called
before we came

                   mother says nudging
                   my bottles back
                   below the bed

me covered in bugs
in my brain again.
hear the clear bell

                   ringing anyway
                   this is where
                   the line breaks
                   down

weeping

                   for no reason
                   other than the beauty
                   of the page   pause

where a staggered
thought meets

                    the profound metered
                    evenness of the world
the world
at rest. any disease
of the mind traced

                    back to its origin
                    is a sickle
is silk

                    it's sick isn't it?

#MANIA

we're not on speaking terms

i shout curses into the skeletal
awnings of pay phones

parking meters vomit coins
as i pass : mad presidents

at my feet, embossed
in silver & nickel & copper

the sewer grate's yawning
in the floodwaters

i take my shelter where i can
get it   dance in the street

light's spotlight. move so quick
even rain can't get me wet

text everyone—everyone text
get a few messages back

spread me across the city   tonight
finds us in a man's apartment

with a bottle of old crow deranged
& flapping blackly below my jacket

i take my shelter where i can
get it   his face is full of puncture

wounds & dead stars shine
through him   tonight i don't have

a father no matter what
this man wants me to call him

when the street greets me after
i'm half calamity & half bitter cream

i am beating the morning forward
with the wilderness of my sneakers

i am belting unbearable songs
from the penthouse of my lungs

i am taking my shelter & tearing it
open in my gums

i am watching my father spill out of me
all over this city's waking radios

KLONOPIN

a doctor names the chemical imbalance in my brain
& suddenly there's an infant wailing up there.
i swear the cradle appeared concomitant
with the diagnosis, a migraine-white mobile wail.
i say moderation is a red swamp i'm always bicycling
toward, it recedes the more i believe in it. you say
it's a simple swallowing & flood, the pram an ark
afloat in the choking basement. angels slum
in the aggregate gray matter as i wait for the sitter
to finish smothering the child. when it's quiet
i name all the wet little rooms in my head after
dead poets. i name the burst water pipes in the walls.
i name the electricity. this is just to say, i have eaten
all the pills i've been prescribed & am nothing
                                        now. forgive me.

WARNING : RED LIQUID

don't ask why
i nearly emptied the saccharine flask
                   opiates & homatropine testing
my limits

you either love the world
or you live in it

all my poems are wild birds
        pecking eyeholes in the windows of hotels

in california there are no seasons
        still you find a way to be sad all year round

seasonless affective disorder
no one calls it

but me

just now

say cathedral & mean simply a building
        you take shelter behind to light a cigarette
say love & mean a man
                        moving through you like water
how he turns undrinkable
                soon as he leaves your body

i carry much nostalgia for the times i don't remember

the evening ritual of breaking
        rolling & smoking a small kingdom
                        liquor-man with my name on his breath
call from a lost friend full of unfamiliar stories
                me in all of them

those years i was lonely
          as a window even the light refused
to pass through

don't ask me to name the precise strain of terror so elemental
          it throbbed   how the organs in my stomach became strange
the grope of cement i woke twitching against

near death is how you tell it

outside my window children beat fake animals
hanging from the trees with metal bats

i take out the bottle

inside my body
                    a white door
          opens into a room
full of red-faced men
                              blood moons
the lot of them

don't ask me why i kept it
the bottle

i'll lie

MEMORIAL SLOAN KETTERING CANCER CENTER

the sick are taken
for walks around the hospital

fourteen laps is a mile
we make it six

the ones in yellow socks are dying
the ones in gray are dying
slower

last week he was attached
to so many tubes he was
an oldsmobile trailing
wedding cans

today his friend left
room 1634 in a hearse
vanished and we say
he went home

we pass a body bag and i'm convinced
it's closed because the corpse is hideous

if the body were beautiful in death
we'd lay us out upon pavilions
we'd braid us ashes into our hair

my uncle's so drugged he hardly remembers
i'm here, the bite of the catheter pulled out,
the unassassinated breath, daydreams of insects

we walk past the painting of a boy
holding flowers and then that same
painting again and again

his wound is a mile long across
sutured with a string
his body will eat as it heals

it's really something, he says, looking
at the child as if he's never seen it,

*the way the sounds of ecstasy
are the same as the sounds of pain . . .
put that in a poem,*

i nod my head, pretend
i've never thought this

that i haven't had a man
reach inside me to grip
the yardstick of my spine and smile
at the sounds i made

at apogee the moon is 252,088 miles away

the sick walk circuits
retrace the dead's footsteps
march toward them

HEMATOLOGY

while he lives

here's a list

of images :

light in a filthy glass

pigeon dead on the high spiked window

clear plastic bag above him full of water if water could kill

everything that lives in you & it can—

i sit in a corner of the cancer ward

fingering the app that shows me

other faggots in this hospital

chat with one

i might meet in radiology

but don't   instead

make the sick man laugh

while he's conscious

compliment his gown

his new brutal cheekbone

that appeared with the chemo

if only it were simple as a magnet

sucking the bad metals out of him

if only i could make a better list

more magic   less language

periphrastic & restorative

if only i met that stranger

in the basement

& our pleasure rose

through the hospital

bliss poultice

for the sorrow-skinned who sit

half-conscious & half-machinery

while the sick man lives

all i can do is recount

the vast pastoral of his illness

when he is gone i'm counting

on all the good flooding back

his beard

a collapsed country

i'll refuge inside

his laugh

a memory

so liquid

i'll hear it

when anyone

opens a window

to scare the birds

thirst curtain   dirt curtsy.
cursed & forever bursting
at the seams. at the cement truck
with   my   mouth   open.
my tongue tongues my name
into the wet, into the forever
hardening. at   the   mouth
of the river with my mouth
open, all the fishies & oil spills
in.   all the rowboats float clean
into harbor. once a man ran
his hand across my lower back
& everything that followed was
sampled music. bloated & au
naturel. o pathology, come filter
clean   these   killing   fields.
dear diseases with greek names,
deer in velvet bent over in a field
of felled trees, dear all—philias
& the most beloved felt-up
bearded stomachs—i ask to be
fucked by every terrible brilliant
thing at once. i am large.
i contain mitochondria clubbed
into cells, i contain blue
cellophane shoved in my mouth,
i contain unnatural lubricants,
the smell of latex & fennel. o
doctor, what a white coat you

have. o father what sweet rope. o government how absurd to believe desire requires governance. keep giving lust an ugly name, i'll keep making it sing. my number's written on every bathroom stall from here to here.

THE SURGEON

thumbs the organ open
bulbous & cultivated
gloved index kneading
the liver the liver the liver.
on the other side of the skin
partition the surgeon knows
nothing of living. when
he looks at his wife, she smiles
& he watches each muscle
volt into place. the surgeon
became the surgeon after
years of opening
books & making sense
of their contents, of apprenticing
at the feet of learned men,
of learning the gestures
of confidence that must be
performed with both hands
buried inside another person.
my uncle's unconscious
the anesthesiologist has fed
him to the chemical fog,
slowed his heart rate down
to the bold clot of hibernation.
his children still patient
are home making each other
eggs & bleed. my uncle

became my uncle through sex
& greed. my uncle became
sick for no good reason
other than the anthropocene.
the bright room's full
of professionals nodding
their hoarse nurse heads.
admiring the surgeon & his
machine-quality wrists,
his sweat-dappled grimace.
this is the fifth of this kind
this morning & each man
has a family at home who carry
their sicknesses like little
batteries leaking in flashlights.
on the operating table
the surgeon peels each man
back careful as a leather-bound
bible & all the dead letters,
all the generations experimented
upon, the enslaved & saved
alike are there, before
our interiority finally clicked
into place. once, before science
drew its maps, you might have cut
open a dead man's stomach
& watched a masque of old horses
come dancing out.

ON PREP OR ON PRAYER

high risk factors

+ inconsistent condom use;

         i slip

+ sexual contact associated with substance abuse;

         my arm

+ history of prior STI;

         into the earth

+ anonymous sexual partner(s);

         & pull out

+ multiple sexual partners (> 1 per year);

         the fat heart

+ forced/coerced sexual contact;

         of a deer

+ history of tattoo;

         shot through

+ history of MSM;

         the stomach

+ sexual contact with known positive HIV partner(s);

         by famine

+ sexual contact with known IV drug use by patient or partner(s);

         & watch how

+ history of body piercing;

         it still

+ history of shared razors;

         throbs

AT E

APPENDIX C OF THE *DSM-I* (1952)

SUPPLEMENTARY TERMS OF THE BODY AS A WHOLE (INCLUDING
SUPPLEMENTARY TERMS OF THE PSYCHE AND OF THE BODY
GENERALLY) AND THOSE NOT AFFECTING A PARTICULAR SYSTEM
EXCLUSIVELY

order / disorder

Acarophobia – Acrophobia – Agoraphobia – Antisocialism – Anxiety
– Asthenia – Breath holding – Bruxism – Cachexia – Cancerophobia
– Causalgia – Claustrophobia – Cheiromegaly (enlargement of hands
and fingers) – Chills – Chilly sensations – Collapse – Counting (steps,
etc.) – Cruelty – Deficiency, moral – Dehydration – Delire de toucher
– Depersonalization – Depression – Destructiveness – Diabetes insipidus
– Dipsomania – Disobedience – Edema, hysterical – Edema, other
types – Emotional instability – Enuresis – Erotomania – Facetiousness
– Fatigue, abnormal – Fears, mixed – Feeding problem in children –
Folie du doute – Forgery – Fugue – Gain in weight – Homosexuality –
Hypothermia – Kleptomania – Loss in weight – Mania – Masturbation
– Mendacity pathologic: untruthfulness – Misanthropy – Misogyny –
Moria (Witzelsucht) – Mysophobia – Nail biting – Negativism –
Nymphomania – Obesity – Overactivity – Pain, general – Panic – Panic,
acute homosexual – Paranoid trends – Paroxysmal automatism –
Paroxysmal clouded states – Paroxysmal furor – Paroxysmal psychic
equivalents – Personality, dual – Personality, dissociated – Personality,
paranoid – Personality, schizoid – Personality, syntonic –
Phthisiophobia – Pyrexia; hyperthermia – Pyromania; setting fires –
Quarrelsomeness – Sexual immaturity – Sex offenses – Sexual perversion
– Shock – Simulation, malingering – Somnambulism – Somniloquism
– Stealing – Syncope – Syphilophobia – Tantrums – Tetany – Tetany
due to hyperventilation – Thumb sucking – Tongue swallowing –
Trance – Trichokryptomania – Trichotillomania – Truancy – Urge to
say words – Use of alcohol – Use of drugs – Vagabondage – Vagrancy

grandpa collects german expressionist prints & hangs them

on his walls like the severed stuffed heads of animals.   o

the animals, the animals.   there's one, a purple woman,

wraith in her wide sun hat who's haunted me through

my youth—face caught between two paralytic worlds.

there's another of an old man hauling wheat up an impossible

slope for all eternity. i ask my grandfather about this obsession,

the impulse to collect the grotesque & display it. the woodcut,

the lithograph, the etching. their black frames   a cage to master

the monster or harvest what's left untorched—while studying

to become a therapist his anti-semitic teacher had a single

german print hanging from a nail in his office & the nail sang.

my grandfather decided then & there to collect everything.

nagging awful art. sick selfish city of art. wall of colony &

recrimination. curator of the barbarous zoo. nolde's deranged face cut into wood, then reproduced in ink—i lived with a man

for a time who collected exotic soaps. my rent, an evening bath.

o   the animals, the animals reduced to fats & famish. o

the urge to become the collected thing, the safety of being kept

& shelved amidst your siblings. i'd rather not talk anymore

about that man, only use him as a window out of the poem :

the alienist, hauling his horror-prints up that impossible slope.

ON SYPHILIS

while it lives in me i imagine the shepherd leading his ghost flock
through the impossible futurity of my nervous system

at the clinic the nurse empties her syringe into the meat
of my left ass cheek

i walk through the waiting room winking at the shook boys
preparing for their sentence

::

i've begun to grow distrustful of sense
the way a poem makes its borders
the well-ordered object   says *this is what i mean*
means it.

artificial little windmill   :   faux revelation   :   replica godhead

let there be madness in the text

sheets of metal   sheets of music

::

syphilis has its origins in empire

the myths that bring it to literature are all based on a distrust
of others   the boats that ferried it back across the atlantic

trailing rags & blankets   the port's mouth that grows rabid
& rashes & loses its nose   depending where you are

it's always from elsewhere

::

before penicillin, sufferers wore their affliction

                black pit in the middle of the face, a door

for a time it was chic : poxed & monstrous mark of the beast

        rash & pestilence, a new garment

::

the name we use today was given to us by a poem

follows a young shepherd named syphilus, who became the microbe

the strangest plague returned to sear the world

::

bacteria infiltrates the brain & [re-]creates psychosis

the first cure was mercury injected directly into the blood

psychiatrists engineered fevers

injected streptococcus, tuberculin, malaria

::

there's something exquisite knowing without sex this illness
would not exist   i did not receive this perspective

with my diagnosis   the countless human houses the strain
must have passed through in order to move into me—to shut

off the water & electricity   you could fill a whole complex
with that family

::

perhaps my sickness is descendant of the same animal that warred
          in my ancestry during the last great war

perhaps it's the same as keats's wandering insane through europe
          with blood in his teeth

::

at the tuskegee institute the u.s. government conducted
a forty-year syphilis study of black sharecroppers, monitoring
& refusing to offer treatment

the bacteria spread like a religion through their families

as a part of the study the government provided free burial insurance

::

i know the easy method of treatment metered out to me
comes directly from their suffering

i know all things are this way

a single injection trails with it hundreds of thousands of sick
wrapped in heated blankets, electrocuted, & poisoned to sweat
out their madness

stare at any serum long enough, it unbraids

ON HYSTERIA

hippocrates believed the uterus
moved freely around the body

little hitchhiker with her thumb out
on the highway of the small intestine

she visits the various organs

she brings her whiskey

    ::

the cure for a woman suffering
hysteria was once to be masturbated
by a professional

the doctor's dumb gloved hand

the metal table

stirrups

    ::

hippocrates was a mthfkr

    ::

my grandfather   the psychotherapist
was alive & working during this time

i asked him about the practice

he smiled

said everyone left feeling better

::

the first time a doctor entered me
had nothing to do with madness
or pleasure

his camera the size of a thumb
was a steam engine
piercing the desert

he was searching my ass
for polyps

for signs of signs of infection

sweat on his forehead
lip turned up at the edge

::

what does it mean to be descendant
of something monstrous?

to still love the monster?

::

the vibrator was invented
to serve doctors
who serviced hysterical women

their poor corpsed hands
clenched & extinguished
with each orgasm

their sad dour countenance

poor poor doctors
in over their heads

    ::

across the house

i can still hear

my mother gasp

against the sound

of shaking metal

    ::

it's beautiful
how technology can move
from its corrupt origins
into pleasure

i have to remember the internet
began inside the murder
corridors of a war machine

each time i link to a poem
or watch two queers kiss

    ::

there's a photograph
of my grandfather holding me
after an asthma attack
until my breathing evened out again

::

i'm sick for this

but need to ask if surgery
isn't a kind of intercourse

the making of a new orifice
the insertion of instruments
into the body

::

my grandfather's a good man
my grandfather was accused of [   ]

both these things are true

::

before science

could peer inside

the body nothing

was fixed. all our

organs floated &

changed form.

the heart & brain

two dark forests

ON MASS HYSTERIA

goya, the painter, believed
there is no difference
between the insanity
of the asylum & the insanity
of the crowd

::

when i say mass i mean of course
a gathering of bodies

when i say mass of course
i mean a gathering for prayer

::

at a demonstration in oakland
to protest the light sentence
of oscar grant's murderer

i stood in a crowd of many white
faces shouting—i am oscar grant

a handful were wearing white paper
masks printed with an image
of the dead black man's face

::

on the train earlier that day
i nodded at a policeman
& the policeman nodded back

::

goya, the painter, painted
the same figure into two paintings

dark man with a pained face
pointed up at god

in one he's in a parade
drowning in celebration

in the other he's in a madhouse
holding the whip

::

the grasshopper's oft mistook
for the locust

it's believed when they gather
in swarms a chemical changes their brain
& makes them want to eat the world

::

goya, the painter, is begging
the question

who's more deranged
the viewer or subject?

who carries the wound
the one who wields the lash
or the one who bears it?

::

when i say mass
i also mean the quantity
of matter in a body

::

i cannot see a white crowd
& not not look to history

not not see all the mad
reasons people gather

::

in 1500s strasbourg a plague broke out
where the victims suffered dancing

it's funny until you learn
there was no end

until you look at the figures
of how many dead

::

perhaps mass hysteria
is a cousin of empathy.
your neighbor weeps
so you weep. your neighbor
needs a man dead
so you kill him.

::

in the catholic tradition
the congregation participates
in the collective delusion
of eating the body of their god

but none would dare say

         i am jesus christ

::

men strung up like cans of paint

witches drowned in the river

the bomb dropped upon your own city

riots that followed the rites of spring

riots that follow the giants' victory

::

perhaps empathy's nothing more
than your junkie cousin

who spends the night only to run
off with your black & white tv

::

perhaps we should let the locusts
swarm the museums, eat the wheat fields
from all the dead painters' paintings

::

even as a child

i felt the pulse

quicken in my neck

as the crowd

surged around

two boys

fists clenched

trying to paint

the other

the other red

ON TREPANATION

logic at its root is a medical instrument.

::

ten percent of human skulls recovered from the stone age have silver dollar sized holes bored out of them. the bone removed. the button opened.

::

the tools they must have used to perform this surgery were crude, rock-made, rudimentary, ignoble implements. must have had good reason.

::

the brain swells to twice its size just thinking of it.

::

surely their logic was a logic of monsters. the way a demon takes up residence in the gray matter. builds a haunt shack below the bridge of your nose & through the bored hole said demon can be released from its captive inelastic concavity.

::

the homosexual since his invention has been a creature held captive in the skull.

::

simple ritual : touch the back of your head. invent an absence in the solid matter. trace the serrated ridge. imagine what might come sprinting from your head if only you had the acumen to drill a hole in it.

::

athena was born this way.

phineas gage is said to have had a metal rod pass through his brain
& emerge out the other side a swan.

in the film π the hero learns the true name of god by opening
his occipital bone.

::

every instrument of torture is born this way. every instrument
of sound & surgery. every painting & chair & chariot. every ritual
& rite of passage. every word & hermeneutic.

::

the skulls of fetuses come soft & in pieces so they can pass easier
through their mothers into the world. the fontanels harden with age
until behold your new adult shape.

::

perhaps that ancient surgery is less about monsters & more of an
argument for the preservation of youth. to break apart the skull
so you might pass back through your mother into oblivion.

::

i understood this smoking cigarette after cigarette on the front porch
of a man who'd gripped my head as if he were trying to disassemble it.
how much easier it would have been had he succeeded. smoke rising
up through the hole in me.

::

after, i lay beside him in the position all humans take preparing
for sleep regardless of age, or history, of what terrible things
they've just done with their hands.

ON ALCOHOL

my first drink was in my mother
my next, my bris. doctor spread red
wine across my lips. took my foreskin

::

every time i drink   i lose something

::

no one knows the origins of alcohol. tho surely an accident
before sacrament. agricultural apocrypha. enough grain stored up
for it to get weird in the cistern. rot gospel. god water.

::

brandy was used to treat everything
from colds to pneumonia
frostbite to snakebites

tb patients were placed on ethanol drips
tonics & cough medicines
spooned into the crying mouths of children

::

each friday in synagogue a prayer for red
at dinner, the cemetery, the kitchen
spirits

::

how many times have i woke
strange in an unfamiliar bed?
my head neolithic

::

my grandfather died with a bottle in one hand
& flowers in the other. he called his drink his medicine
he called his woman
                    she locked the door

::

i can only half-blame alcohol for my overdose
the other half is my own hand
that poured the codeine   that lifted the red plastic again & again &

::

i'm trying to understand pleasure   it comes back
in flashes   every jean button thumbed open to reveal
a different man   every slurred & furious permission

::

i was sober a year before [   ] died

::

every time i drink   i lose someone

::

if you look close at the process of fermentation
you'll see tiny animals destroying the living body
until it's transformed into something more volatile

::

the wino outside the liquor store
mistakes me for his son

ON CONVERSION THERAPY

grandpa's initial response
upon learning i was queer
was to look to history
for the ways i could be fixed

::

hypnosis : group talk : cocaine : bladder washing : electroconvulsive
shock therapy : strychnine : chemical & nonchemical castration :
rectal massage : bicycling : institutionalization : inducing vomit
while looking at homoerotic images : orgasmic reconditioning :
cold showers : prayer : satiation therapy : psychotropic medicines.

::

the first endocrinologist experimenting in the field
transplanted the testicles of straight men into homosexuals
attempting to hormonally reorder their orientation.
of course without immunosuppressants their bodies
rejected these unfamiliar organs.

::

all precious stones are made this way
through a process of applied heat & pressure

::

even now we know queerness
                          is a kind of possession
dybbuk-headed thirst
thirst-headed dybbuk

                    the priest replaced by the therapist
the swallow-quiet exorcism

::

as a boy i held a woman for a time
& her body was a rejected organ
in my hands

what i mean is once i was a boy

::

of course i tried to take my life
into my own hands

       choir of children's tylenol
       all singing joy to the world

       the knife singing an older song

       the liquor the liquor

::

family is the mineral vein
& love is the hand that polishes

who gives a damn
about my forgiveness

::

there's nothing innate in the brain
about the objects we lust after

when i attempt to place my tongue
on the root of desire
it ends up torn out of my mouth

::

before the advent of analysis
faggots were either gods or monsters
either ended in jail or in pleasure
in heaven or in flames

when i say pre-exposure prophylaxis

you think

> easy fix. greek in origin. an act of guarding.
> east of here a small temple
> inside parishioners strip nude
> as armless statues, their stone
> genitals hardening under a chemist's glare.
> the garden out front fecund & tended.
> the garden inside bare.

when i say tenofovir disoproxil

you think

> chemical names. saint names. names without origin.
> an unpronounceable string of letters. the generic names
> of petty angels. the drug's molecular makeup applied in
> & around the eyes & lips. the names of viruses & blind trials.
> the kept-vial of love. the unknowable side effects of blood.

when i say oral emtricitabine

you think

> once a day swallow a small sun
> & all hymn in you comes undone
>
> the way a lit match deads the smell
> of a public bathroom

when i say nucleotide analog reverse-transcriptase inhibitor

you think

thirsty epidemic
you push the blue pill through its foil

you know each new medicine trails
our dead behind it like wedding cans

listen
you can hear them now, can't you?

N   ATURE

-I (   )

(

)

/

             –   –   –   –

–   –   –   –   –

–   –   –   (

)   –   –   (,

.)–   –   ,   –   –

–   –   –   –

–   –   –   ,   –   ,

–   –   –   –

–   ,   –   ,   –   –

–   –   –   –

–   –   –   –

–   :   –   –   –

(   )–   –   –

–   –   –   ,   –   –   ,

–   –   –

–   ,   –   ,   –   ,

–   ,   –   ,   –

–   ;   –   ;   –

–   –   –

–   –   ,   –   –

–   –   –   –

        –   –   –

      –   –   –

–   –   –

PSYCHOTHERAPY

what brings you here today?

    hear the sickle blood quicken
    here, a billion muscles bilging lungs

have you seen a counselor before?

    there's always been a shadow-man in my past
    there'll always be men in shadows ahead

    i'll only speak of the vagabonds
    the baddest exes, the already dead

is there a history of mental illness in your family?

    some questions are best answered
        with silence. fear is a superior cancer
  to cancer. the brain cantors in its chemical
        bath. each invisible aphid swarming
  the trauma ports, passing through the blood
        harbor, leaving you this new new
    dance: an evolutionary flinch that happens
        when anyone asks you to tell
  about your family.

what is the problem from your viewpoint?

    i forgot there are rivers /
                that aren't filled with garbage

    city rivers. concrete filthy rivers. rivers that run
    off from their factories & join the current. chemical rivers.
    rivers of medical waste. ecumenical rivers. rivers of paint
    & rivers of blood & rivers of saints & rivers of drugs.
    rivers of whiskey i've drunk & pissed into rivers & rivers

of depressed syringes & rivers children wade into
& don't return from children

how does this make you feel?

    o the teethed root structures of trees
        o the beetle-nosed murder economy
    o the beehive drooling gasoline

    o the vermin with opal & gold fronted teeth
        o the airplane's blueprinted hate speech
    o the wind that passes through cities & leaves

    o the wind that's been touched & touches
    but has no memory

what do you expect from the counseling process?

    i once believed you could split open
    the spine of a book & find a synopsis

    i once believed the foundations of libraries
    were built from felled trees

    i once believed the written word
    could survive death

    i once believed survival had something
    to do with language

tell me about your mother?

    are you my mother? i ask the lake
    black ink spill i lower my hands into
    only to have them disappear

are you my mother? i ask the sky
& the clouds only reflect down
light pollution

are you my mother? i ask my body in the dark
& a grown woman emerges from my head

are you my mother? i ask my mother
she laughs & i ask again

overall how would you describe your mood?

there must be something else
worth praising besides pleasure
& destruction

what do you think it would take to make you feel better?

you take what you can

take what you can take

what you can take what

you can take what you

can take what you can

POSTDIAGNOSIS

REASON / *UNREASON*

the brain is

easily charted

using machines

& therapy

don't worry

your pretty head

it's simple

to manage

with the appropriate

medicines

an unlit synagogue

in dark waters

it can baffle faith

it can asphyxiate

the drowning dogs

painted for the gods

to rage & riot & rot

the vacant parking lot

knives   do what some

cannot

FAIRY TALE

a boy's kicked out of his house
so he moves into the baths
+ becomes the steam
men breathe in + out again
+ this is a kind of homecoming,
tendriled in these new lung
gutters, aqueduct full + emptying
of mucus + curses. *god*
as he passes through a hand
clamped over a drooling mouth.
god as he's sucked back up
inside a body. can you believe
there's freedom in being so out
of control you can pass through
a man unseen, lie dormant
as an idea or disease until
you reemerge years later
through his speech or semen?
in this way the men bring him
into their homes, kiss him
onto their wives' + children's
sleeping foreheads. in this way,
the boy is everywhere + everywhere
is the boy. sort of how matter
can never be created or destroyed,
that same idea, just much
much sadder.

MIASMA

of course when the plague came
those who could
left the city

the wealthy
burdened their horses
with precious stones
& dead flowers
—left their houses
bolted & prayed for

while gone
they burdened their children
with stories of a homeland
before it'd fallen
into the teeth of rats

with the doctors gone
anyone who wanted
could treat the sick
how they wanted

wear a bird mask
dark cloak & a cane
to prod the abrasions
deviling across
the sufferings' back

it's an old story, one world
ends & a man gets rich
selling the copper wire
in the walls

another flips a quarter
& buys the flooded
neighborhood

another patents a medicine
old as the earth

it was once believed illness
was a punishment
from god

now we have machines
that show the small crow
shaped tumors growing
in my grandmother's brain

now my uncle can have
an irradiated vein planted
just above his heart

a doctor pads his white
coat with bones until it flairs
into wings

when the children
returned to their city

they found their houses
filled with birds, birds,
birds

all the old cruising spots have been transformed into parks
again, the hole in the bathroom stall condemned & patched,
the bathhouse palace palanquin of ghosts. when we are done
all that's left behind us are facts. the ground's been turned over
so much by commerce & colony you'd think it was my father
turning in his sleep—worried about the kind of man i was
out with that evening. i'd like to believe the soil remembers us,
that all that semen grew something :

>   a statue in the shape of a syringe
>   a marble-wet trembling bottom lip

there's a reason the flowers
in fukushima grow two-headed

that this whole godforsaken country's tumored over
with fast food & faster cars

white gentlemen in black finery sit in a raked amphitheater to watch keats hold a woman down while an infant is cut unsuccessfully out of her. no one lives. none of them know keats & none of them will. the scalpels gleam silver & crimson. the doctor's procedure is filled with latin & greek names for the body. i don't care much for keats but know his work. it's been passed down, a dominant gene, each line canonical & diagrammed in books until they're stripped of life, two-dimensional representation of a once living thing. the cesarean gets its name not from caesar but rather the latin *caedere*, to cut. *et tu, brute?* every myth has its eponymous origin. every corpse laid prostrate & slit for wealthy gentlemen to gaze into & see their futures. every peoples have been paraded before white men in the name of science, been caged & splayed & made unliving in books & in life & in glass jars. in the beginning western medicine was a human heart drinking formaldehyde. no, in the beginning the bodies of saints were autopsied to see how their organs differed from our own. no, the beginning was a dark auditorium giving birth to more darkness, a new analgesic cut from a suffering body, a desperate woman with her hands in the earth willing to do anything to save her child.

#MELANCHOLIA

you're sad again & everyone can tell.
sadness hath been visited upon your face.

dumb face can't even keep to itself.
your mouth a weird brand of suffering.

when sadness comes to your doorstep
he brings a newspaper cone of dead

rhododendrons, he's already eaten
the blooms. you put the stems

in porcelain anyways, invite him in.
when he's all moved inside you

let the world know. you say, i am sad,
to anyone inquiring into the time

or directions to the subway. you say,
i am sad, & it's not so much

a weight as a series of levers pulling
the meat around. not so much a place

as the edge of map slowly being eaten
by flames. your therapist doesn't want you

to start from the beginning again. instead
focus on manageable steps. from here to

the refrigerator, from there to your flight
out of town. best have some lamb's blood

spread across the front door so the next time
sadness comes, he'll pass over your house

& into your neighbor's son. you in your
wedding dress weeping on the front stoop,

ass peeking out below that white storm cloud.
or maybe it's time for the pills. chemicals

your brain's been aching for since learning
their existence, a boy you fell in love with

on television & stalked online until he grew
drugged out into a thin line then dead.

no one carries the already drowned out
of the river unless they cared for the body

while it lived. i'm standing at the edge
of the river & naming all the garbage

floating past, my sadness. the bodies,
the bodies, my sadness. the boats

& the bloated animals & the broken-in
houses, mine.

shiver thin the winter's thievery. give that feeling a name. pray at it.

on the porch you can just make out the corpses of trees waving
their dark fingers as you turn the flame up to make smoke rise
unmetered from the glass.

old ritual you've returned to now you're deconstituted. desperate
little diagram trying to make sense of a man's absence & the
        hormones quarreling in the skull.

now there's just a pit in the midst of you & the only thing you can
think to fill it with is dogs but of course you haven't got any left

instead make yourself a blazon   scatter of limb & image
& isn't this what you're scared of most   to be seen   in pieces
to matter   then martyr   then disappear completely.

& aren't you too old to have a drug problem anyway & aren't
those dogs too pretty & leashed to be stray

the painkillers you brought from california are barking in the cabinet
they sound good together & not so faint as they once did when
all your clothing was folded & sorted by color. & maybe this man
really did break your heart & you didn't just use the pit he left
as an on-ramp back toward obliteration.

driving home you feel the liquor guide your hands through the blood
greedy streets. you feel the pressure in your feet make the car leap
forward as if you owned something. invite any man over
no matter how much he's had to drink

> *you have a pretty mouth & hair*
> *& eyes & mouth & mouth*

whatever happens next
you deserve it

THEIA MANIA

plato said some shit
& here we are

rats in chemical rapture
drones of light

this state of mind
a fevered state
a matter of nation

i know no god
but am frenzied

by all of them

every morning
we stand

hand over heart

in praise of a flag
stitched together
by enslaved women

every book burning
only exists

if the flames are
remembered or recorded

every anthem
sung is a scythe of birds
graphing the sky

love at first sight
is only possible
if the government

hasn't first
taken your eyes

A.S.H. CEMETERY [AUSTIN, TEXAS]

they buried the unclaimed nameless in a field
       just north of the city & the city grew around it

no monuments mark those below the grasses
       could be a park if they ever unlocked the gate

the unclaimed came from the hospital back
       when the hospital was called an asylum

what else changed with our language?

what's come from all our progress? all our progression
       from animal into angel into engine?
              what of all our invasive photographs of the brain?

there are potter's fields everywhere & the bodies stay
       until flood or famine or gentrification

maybe in death all our madness leaches
       with our plastics into the soil; maybe the worms
          do the worm in the earth

each grave is the ground sobbing open:
       someone might put in a poem

but for their burials the ritual was surely stripped
       of its pomp & pageantry

no widow left to mourn
       & if there was she left long ago

perhaps a few words in latin then the earth shoveled back
       into the earth

today i watched a man cut the lawn smooth as a bedsheet
       from atop his high-powered machine

every blade of grass is a headstone
              they grow despite us

ERASURE

erase the railroad that brought the trains here. erase the trains
& their antique machinery. erase the saloons & the syphilis.
erase the families that settled this stretch of desert & called it
uninhabited. erase the conquered families, cities, &
civilizations. erase the conquerors & erase their horses. erase
the documentary exploring the history of this region on my
computer. erase my computer & all the lives it lets me visit
but not die in. erase the website where i can follow the
satellite's many-eyed lens into my family's gray yard & see only
pixels. erase the amateur video of the couple fucking in
another tab & especially erase the moment where one whispers
something unintelligible into the other's dark ear & the body
shudders. erase the video still open of the man being choked
to death by police less i, in my whiteness, forget it. erase the
last line for the privileged detachment of its witness. erase my
body sitting at this table erasing through accumulation. erase
the many diseases of its mind, its obsession with pleasure &
more pleasure, each addiction replaced by another addiction,
a door opening into a hospital of doors. erase its fugues &
hubris & melancholia. erase its dysthymia & mania & chronic
insomnia. in the beginning there was a word tortured into
birthing new words. & here we sit at the prow of a great ship
cutting through text so thick it resembles black water. here
is the curtain opening its throat to reveal a pair of scissors:
the railroad syphilis.   the horse computers.   the satellite
fucking the other's dark ear.   the video hospital.   the mind
tortured into curtains.   curtain.

ACKNOWLEDGMENTS

Thanks to the editors of the following journals, who published these poems in one version or another:

AGNI: "Memorial Sloan Kettering Cancer Center"; *American Literary Review*: "Psychotherapy [the therapist]"; *The American Poetry Review*: "Erasure"; *The Baffler*: "Sanctuary"; *BOAAT*: "#Melancholia"; *Black Warrior Review*: "Satyriasis"; *BuzzFeed*: "Fairy Tale"; *FIELD*: "Fever Therapy," "Transorbital Lobotomy"; *Eleven Eleven*: "Klonopin," "On Hysteria"; *Gulf Coast*: "On Conversion Therapy," "On Prep or on Prayer [high risk factors]"; *Indiana Review*: "On Mass Hysteria," "Psychotherapy [what brings you]"; *The Iowa Review*: "Miasma"; *Kenyon Review*: "Theia Mania"; *Poetry*: "Hematology," "On Alcohol," "On Prep or on Prayer [spare us]," "On Prep or on Prayer [when i say]"; *Prairie Schooner*: "Willowbrook"; *Prelude*: "Generational Memory," "Seasonal Affective Disorder"; *RHINO Poetry*: "Post-diagnosis"; *Southern Humanities Review*: "Warning : Red Liquid"; *The Southern Review*: "#Mania"; *Waxwing*: "Diagnosis," "Psychotherapy [i invent]"; *Winter Tangerine Review*: "A.S.H. Cemetery [Austin, Texas]," "On Trepanation."

My deepest gratitude to Sad Boy Supper Club: Cam Awkward-Rich (for always telling me if something's dumb), Hieu Minh Nguyen (my always first reader), and Danez Smith (for always pushing me toward bravery). Thanks to Franny Choi (for the early and last-minute edits), Nic Alea, Fatimah Asghar, Tatyana Brown, Charif Shanahan, Angel Nafis, Shira Erlichman, Alexander Chee, Saeed Jones, francine j. harris, Ariana Brown, Meg Freitag, Corey Miller, Chen Chen,

Layne Ransom, Mark Cugini, Hanif Willis-Abdurraqib, Arati Warrier, Adam Hamze, Abbey Mei Otis, Jelal Huyler, Ife-Chudeni Oputa, Spitshine (University of Texas at Austin), CalSLAM, the Bay Area slam scene, Joshua Nguyen, Jason Bayani, Joshua Merchant, Natasha Huey, Gabriel Cortez, Taya Kitaysky, Blake Lee and Taylor Pate, F. T. Kola, Morgan Parker, Manissa Maharawal, TheUnREAL: Dusty Rose, the Dunce Apprentice, and Baraka Noel (for making me a writer). To Julia Kolchinsky Dasbach, Laura Eve Engel, Paul Tran, Sara Brickman, Micheal Foulk, Travis Tate, Dobby Gibson, A. Van Jordan, Jane Miller, Kazim Ali, Naomi Shihab Nye, Michael McGriff, Lisa Moore, Jim Magnuson, Dean Young, Lisa Olstein, Heather Christle, Bing Li, Carrie Fountain, D. A. Powell, Patricia Smith, Jericho Brown, and Terrance Hayes (for believing in this book). Thanks to Dr. Sydnee McElroy and Justin at *Sawbones* and to Paul Slovak at Penguin. To Matt Sax, Lauren Weisman, my mom, dad, and grandparents, who always challenge and hold me down. Y'all taught me to look past the word to its meat. Without you this book wouldn't be.

Also big thanks to the following institutions for believing in and supporting my work: the James A. Michener Center for Writers and Blue Mountain Center (where most of these poems were written), Lambda Literary, the Poetry at Round Top festival, Tent: Creative Writing, and the National Endowment for the Arts. And lastly, thank you for taking the time to read my poems.

JOHN ASHBERY
Selected Poems
Self-Portrait in a Convex Mirror

PAUL BEATTY
Joker, Joker, Deuce

JOSHUA BENNETT
The Sobbing School

TED BERRIGAN
The Sonnets

LAUREN BERRY
The Lifting Dress

PHILIP BOOTH
Lifelines: Selected Poems 1950–1999

JULIANNE BUCHSBAUM
The Apothecary's Heir

JIM CARROLL
Fear of Dreaming: The Selected Poems
Living at the Movies
Void of Course

ALISON HAWTHORNE DEMING
Genius Loci
Rope
Stairway to Heaven

CARL DENNIS
Another Reason
Callings
New and Selected Poems 1974–2004
Practical Gods
Ranking the Wishes
Unknown Friends

DIANE DI PRIMA
Loba

STUART DISCHELL
Dig Safe

STEPHEN DOBYNS
Velocities: New and Selected Poems: 1966–1992

EDWARD DORN
Way More West

ROGER FANNING
The Middle Ages

ADAM FOULDS
The Broken Word

CARRIE FOUNTAIN
Burn Lake
Instant Winner

AMY GERSTLER
Crown of Weeds
Dearest Creature
Ghost Girl
Medicine
Nerve Storm
Scattered at Sea

EUGENE GLORIA
Drivers at the Short-Time Motel
Hoodlum Birds
My Favorite Warlord

DEBORA GREGER
By Herself
Desert Fathers, Uranium Daughters
God
In Darwin's Room

Men, Women, and Ghosts
Western Art

TERRANCE HAYES
Hip Logic
How to Be Drawn
Lighthead
Wind in a Box

NATHAN HOKS
The Narrow Circle

ROBERT HUNTER
Sentinel and Other Poems

MARY KARR
Viper Rum

JACK KEROUAC
Book of Blues
Book of Haikus
Book of Sketches

JOANNA KLINK
Circadian
Excerpts from a Secret Prophecy
Raptus

JOANNE KYGER
As Ever: Selected Poems

ANN LAUTERBACH
Hum
If in Time: Selected Poems, 1975–2000
On a Stair
Or to Begin Again
Under the Sign

CORINNE LEE
Plenty

PHILLIS LEVIN
May Day
Mercury
Mr. Memory & Other Poems

PATRICIA LOCKWOOD
Motherland Fatherland Homelandsexuals

WILLIAM LOGAN
Macbeth in Venice
Madame X
Rift of Light
Strange Flesh
The Whispering Gallery

ADRIAN MATEJKA
The Big Smoke
Map to the Stars
Mixology

MICHAEL MCCLURE
Huge Dreams: San Francisco and Beat Poems

ROSE MCLARNEY
Its Day Being Gone

DAVID MELTZER
David's Copy: The Selected Poems of David Meltzer

ROBERT MORGAN
Dark Energy
Terroir

CAROL MUSKE-DUKES
An Octave above Thunder
Red Trousseau
Twin Cities

ALICE NOTLEY
Certain Magical Acts
Culture of One
The Descent of Alette
Disobedience
In the Pines
Mysteries of Small Houses

WILLIE PERDOMO
The Essential Hits of Shorty Bon Bon

LIA PURPURA
It Shouldn't Have Been Beautiful

LAWRENCE RAAB
The History of Forgetting
Visible Signs: New and Selected Poems

BARBARA RAS
The Last Skin
One Hidden Stuff

MICHAEL ROBBINS
Alien vs. Predator
The Second Sex

PATTIANN ROGERS
Generations
Holy Heathen Rhapsody
Quickening Fields
Wayfare

SAM SAX
Madness

ROBYN SCHIFF
A Woman of Property

WILLIAM STOBB
Absentia
Nervous Systems

TRYFON TOLIDES
An Almost Pure Empty Walking

SARAH VAP
Viability

ANNE WALDMAN
Gossamurmur
Kill or Cure
Manatee/Humanity
Structure of the World Compared to a Bubble

JAMES WELCH
Riding the Earthboy 40

PHILIP WHALEN
Overtime: Selected Poems

ROBERT WRIGLEY
Anatomy of Melancholy and Other Poems
Beautiful Country
Box
Earthly Meditations: New and Selected Poems
Lives of the Animals
Reign of Snakes

MARK YAKICH
The Importance of Peeling Potatoes in Ukraine
Unrelated Individuals Forming a Group Waiting to Cross